TRIBES of NATIVE AMERICA

Blackfeet

edited by Marla Felkins Ryan
and Linda Schmittroth

BLACKBIRCH®
PRESS

THOMSON
GALE

San Diego • Detroit • New York • San Francisco • Cleveland
New Haven, Conn. • Waterville, Maine • London • Munich

For more information, contact
The Gale Group, Inc.
27500 Drake Rd.
Farmington Hills, MI 48331-3535
Or you can visit our Internet site at http://www.gale.com

Photo credits: Cover Courtesy of Northwestern University Library; cover © National Archives; cover © Photospin; cover © Perry Jasper Photography; cover © Picturequest; cover © Seattle Post-Intelligencer Collection, Museum of History & Industry; cover © Blackbirch Press Archives; cover © Library of Congress; cover © PhotoDisc; page 5, 6, 12, 16, 17, 20, 22, 24, 25, 26, 27, 29 © nativestock.com; page 6, 19, 21, 28 © CORBIS; page 7 © PhotoDisc; page 8, 10 © Corel Corporation; page 9 © Library of Congress; page 14, 18, 23, 30 © Glenbow Archives; page 15 © National Archives

LIBRARY OF CONGRESS CATALOGING-IN-PUBLICATION DATA

Blackfeet / Marla Felkins Ryan, book editor ; Linda Schmittroth, book editor.
v. cm. — (Tribes of Native America)
Includes bibliographical references and index.
Contents: Name — History — The Baker Massacre — Loss of the buffalo — Religion — Daily life — Customs — Current tribal issues.
ISBN 1-56711-605-1 (alk. paper)
1. Siksika Indians—Juvenile literature. [1. Siksika Indians. 2. Indians of North America—Great Plains. 3. Indians of North America—Prairie Provinces.] I. Ryan, Marla Felkins. II. Schmittroth,
Linda. III. Series.
E99.S54 B58 2003
978.004'973—dc21 2002008667

Printed in United States
10 9 8 7 6 5 4 3 2 1

Table of Contents

• FIRST LOOK •

BLACKFEET

Name

Blackfeet are sometimes called Blackfoot. The people called themselves *Siksika*. It means "blackfeet people," and refers to their dark moccasin soles.

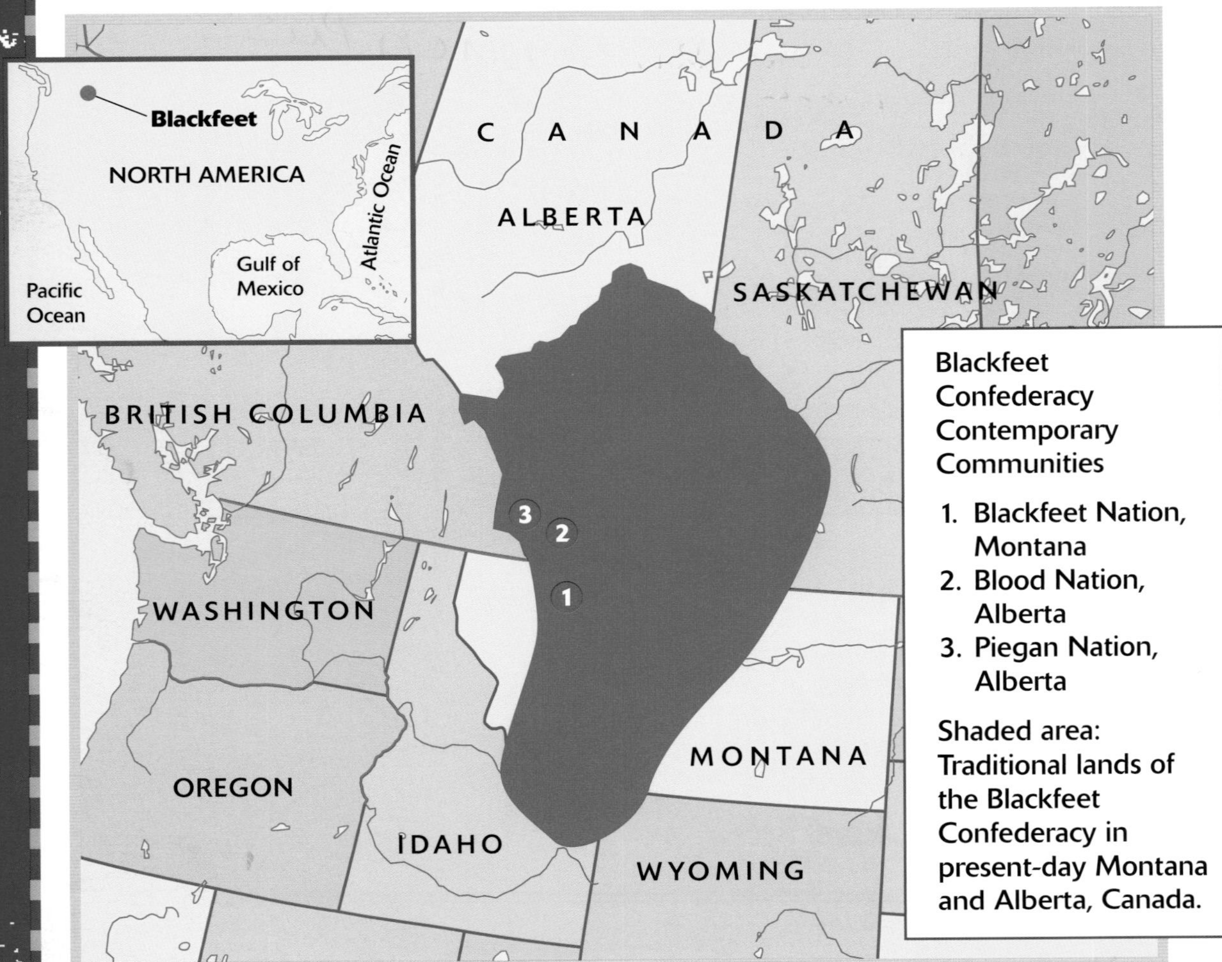

Blackfeet Confederacy Contemporary Communities

1. Blackfeet Nation, Montana
2. Blood Nation, Alberta
3. Piegan Nation, Alberta

Shaded area: Traditional lands of the Blackfeet Confederacy in present-day Montana and Alberta, Canada.

Where are the traditional Blackfeet lands?

The tribes of the Blackfeet lived on the northwestern part of the Great Plains. They lived on land that stretched from the Saskatchewan River in Alberta, Canada, to the headwaters of the Missouri River in Montana. Today, Blackfeet live throughout the United States. Many live in northwestern Montana on the Blackfeet Reservation. Others live in Washington and California. The Blackfeet of Canada live in southeastern Alberta.

A member of the Blackfeet tribe. Blackfeet are sometimes called Blackfoot.

Blackfeet tribes lived along the Saskatchewan River (pictured) in Alberta, Canada.

What has happened to the population?

In the early 1800s, there were about 5,200 Blackfeet. Today, about 15,000 Blackfeet live on three reservations in Canada. About 10,000 live on the Blackfeet Reservation in Montana. In a 1990 population count by the U.S. Bureau of the Census, 37,992 people said they were Blackfeet. This made the tribe the eleventh largest in the United States.

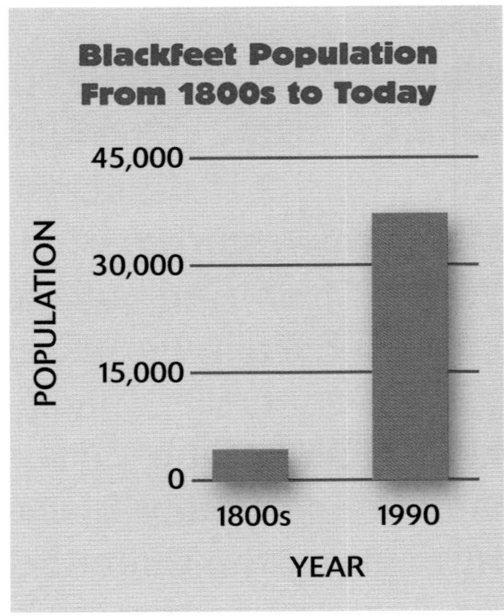

A Blackfeet woman dressed in decorated clothing.

Blackfeet acquired horses in the middle of the 19th century. For centuries, they wandered the plains and hunted buffalo.

Origins and group ties

The Blackfeet Confederacy consists of three tribes who speak the same language and have the same culture. The Piegan's name means "the poorly dressed ones." The Blood, or Kainah, tribe's name means "many chiefs." The Siksika, or Blackfeet proper, are also known as the Northern Blackfeet.

For centuries, the Blackfeet wandered the plains that rise westward to the Rocky Mountains. They hunted buffalo and gathered wild plants. As white settlers moved west, the lives of the Blackfeet changed. The buffalo died off. The Blackfeet died of diseases that the whites carried with them. In modern times, the tribe has fought poverty. It works hard to keep traditions alive.

The Blackfeet wandered across the Great Plains east of the Rocky Mountains.

• Timeline •

1607
English colonists settled Jamestown, Virginia

1620
Mayflower lands at Plymouth, Massachusetts

1776
America declares independence from England

1851
The Treaty of Fort Laramie sets boundaries of Blackfeet territory

1855
Treaty of Lamed Bull offers the Blackfeet goods and education in return for land

1861
American Civil War begins

1865
Civil War ends

1869
Transcontinental Railroad is completed

1870
About 200 Piegan are killed by U.S. soldiers under Major Eugene M. Baker

HISTORY

A powerful tribe

The Blackfeet moved to the Great Plains before the Europeans came. There, the Blackfeet followed the buffalo. They used tame dogs to carry their belongings. This period before they used horses and guns was called the "Dog Days."

The Blackfeet used arrows and spears in wars with the Shoshone, Plains Cree, Flathead, and Assiniboin (pronounced *uh-SIN-uh-boin*). The Blackfeet were friendly with the Gros Ventre (*grow VAHNT*) and Sarsi. The Blackfeet acquired

Blackfeet used weapons such as arrows and spears in wars with other tribes.

Fur trappers first traded goods with the Blackfeet in the 1700s.

1883–1884
Buffalo have almost disappeared. A severe famine strikes, and one-quarter of the Piegan tribe starves

1917–1918
WWI fought in Europe

1929
Stock market crash begins the Great Depression

1934
Indian Recognition Act is passed and the modern economic and political development of the Blackfeet begins

1941
Bombing at Pearl Harbor forces United States into WWII

1945
WWII ends

1950s
Reservations no longer controlled by federal government

horses and guns in the middle of the 18th century. They soon became one of the most powerful tribes of the Northern Plains. By the middle of the 19th century, they had pushed their enemies westward across the Rocky Mountains.

Whites affect the tribe

The first known whites to visit the Blackfeet were fur trappers. They arrived in the middle of the 18th century. The trappers hoped to trade with the Indians. From the whites, the tribe learned about guns. They also were exposed to white diseases. This contact led to smallpox outbreaks in 1781, 1837, and 1869 that killed many Blackfeet.

Blackfeet fight for their lands

In the early 1800s, explorer Meriwether Lewis (1774-1809) met the Blackfeet on one of his trips. He said that the people were strong and honest. They could also be very warlike, though. His party of 8 men was attacked by Blackfeet horse raiders. Lewis and his men managed to flee.

During the 1820s, white trappers tried to take Blackfeet land for themselves. The Blackfeet did

Meriwether Lewis and his men met Blackfeet horse raiders in the early 1800s.

what they could to prevent this. In 1823 alone, Blackfeet killed more than 25 trappers. They stole the guns and supplies of countless others. Eventually, overtrapping greatly reduced the number of beavers. By the end of the 1830s, most white trappers had left the Blackfeet lands. Then, in the 1840s, American settlers began to travel west in large numbers. In the mid-nineteenth century, gold was found near Blackfeet lands. Huge numbers of gold-seekers flooded the whole Blackfeet region.

Treaties limit the Blackfeet

Over the years, the Blackfeet were particularly hostile to Americans. This was in part due to earlier misunderstandings. As they moved west, terrified settlers heard about the Blackfeet's reputation as fierce warriors. They asked the U.S. government to protect them. Whites also wanted Blackfeet land, so the federal government decided to make treaties with the tribe. In time, the tribe lost much of its land in these treaties.

In 1851, the borders of Blackfeet land in the United States were set by the Treaty of Fort Laramie. No Blackfeet took part in the treaty talks. In 1855, the Blackfeet signed their first treaty. It was known as the Treaty of Lamed Bull. This treaty stated that the U.S. government would pay the tribe $20,000 in goods every year. It would also spend $15,000 each

Blackfeet people helped whites to hunt buffalo.

year to educate the Blackfeet and help make them Christians. In return, the Blackfeet gave up half of their hunting land. They agreed to live in peace with their white neighbors. They were also supposed to let white settlers build railroads and telegraph lines.

For a while, relations between the Blackfeet and whites improved. The Blackfeet helped the settlers hunt buffalo. They traded their own buffalo hides for supplies such as beads, guns, wool, wagons, and food. Before long, though, whites began to abuse the treaty. They gave the Indians spoiled food, rusty guns, and blankets with moth holes. The Blackfeet felt disrespected and tricked. They soon responded with anger.

The Baker Massacre

In the 1860s, the Blood tribe of the Blackfeet decided to make a permanent home in Canada to avoid conflicts with whites. They joined the northern Piegan, who had already made the same move. Most of the Blackfeet who stayed in the United States were southern Piegan.

In early 1870, a group of U.S. soldiers attacked the Piegan. This action was called either the Piegan War or the Baker Massacre, named for the American who led the attack. The Piegan involved had never made raids against the whites. In fact, they were weakened from a severe smallpox epidemic. At the time of the attack, most of the Piegan men were away on a hunting trip. The U.S. troops killed 200 Piegan. Most of the victims were women, children, and older people.

Treaties

Treaties signed in 1865 and 1868 decreased the territory of the Blackfeet in the United States. The U.S. Congress never officially confirmed those treaties, though. An 1874 treaty officially set up the Blackfeet Reservation in Montana. The Indians gave up more land from the reservation in treaties signed in 1887 and 1896. The terms of the treaties are still disputed today.

In 1877, with Treaty No. 7, the Canadian government set up reserves in Alberta for the Blood, North Piegan, and Siksika (Blackfeet) people. Canadians wished to avoid Indian wars like those in the United States. They generally treated the natives more fairly and tried to honor their treaties.

Loss of the buffalo

By the 1880s, the buffalo on the Great Plains were almost extinct. White hunters killed the animals in huge numbers for their tongues. Buffalo tongue was considered a treat in Europe. Buffalo were also hunted for their hides, which were made into fashionable clothing. In 1860, factories began to use

The Canadian government and the Blackfeet agreed upon Treaty No. 7 in 1877.

A buffalo hide yard in Dodge City, Kansas. The demand for buffalo hides skyrocketd in the 1860s.

buffalo hide to make machine belts for industry. The price of hides skyrocketed. As a result, the slaughter of the buffalo increased.

Blackfeet in modern times

After the buffalo disappeared, the Blackfeet in Montana faced starvation. From the late 1870s until 1935, the Blackfeet depended on government agencies for food and supplies. They also had to make many cultural changes to adjust to a new farming lifestyle. After 1887, the government divided reservation lands into pieces called allotments. Indians were given small plots of land on which to farm or raise cattle. Many Blackfeet had to give up these lands after a 1919 drought and low beef prices left them unable to pay their taxes.

Modern-day Blackfeet work in ranching and other industries.

In the 1930s, new laws were passed to make the Blackfeet less dependent on the government. Their lands were placed in trust. This meant the government oversaw land use. From 1935 to the 1960s, the Blackfeet became self-sufficient. Today, many people of the Blackfeet Reservation in Montana work in ranching, industry, and oil and natural gas.

Religion

The Blackfeet believed that the physical and supernatural worlds were closely linked. Animals and natural elements had powers that humans could acquire. This transfer of power usually took place in dreams. An animal in human form appeared to the dreamer. It gave him or her a list of objects, songs, and rituals needed to use its power. The dreamer then gathered the objects and placed them in a rawhide pouch. This pouch, called a medicine bundle, was used during social and religious ceremonies.

Medicine bundles held sacred objects and were used during religious ceremonies.

Government

The Blackfeet tribes were divided up into a number of hunting bands. These were led by both war chiefs and civil chiefs. The war chief was chosen because of his reputation as a warrior. The civil chief was chosen for his public-speaking skills.

In 1934, the U.S. Congress passed the Indian Reorganization Act (IRA). It gave back some land to tribes and encouraged self-government on reservations. Today, the affairs of the tribe are run by the Tribal Business Council of the Blackfeet Reservation in Browning, Montana. Its nine members serve two-year terms. The Blackfeet in Canada are run by a single governing body with one chairperson.

Blackfeet chief Crowfoot. Each Blackfeet band was led by several chiefs.

Economy

In early days, the Blackfeet were a wandering people. They depended mostly on hunting, and raised no food. Around 1915, the U.S. government suggested that they try to raise livestock rather than farm. A 1919 drought and a drop in beef prices caused this venture to fail. In the 1920s, a tribal leader encouraged the people to grow grains and vegetables on small farms.

Today, many people grow grains and raise livestock. Others work in construction and the timber industry. About one-third of the people on the reservation work for the tribal government. Nearly 40 percent of jobs are linked to federal government programs, such as the construction of government-funded housing. Small businesses make pens and pencils, tepees, and canvas bags. Coal, oil, and natural gas are present on the reservation, but the mining industry is not yet developed. On the Canadian reserves, Blackfeet make houses, clothing, moccasins, and native crafts.

DAILY LIFE

Families

The typical Blackfeet family was made up of two men, three women, and three children. Men often had more than one wife. This may have been because many Blackfeet men were killed in battle, which left extra women. Second and third wives were usually the sisters of a man's first wife.

Buildings

Because of their hunting lifestyle, the Blackfeet lived in single-family tepees that were easy to build and move. The frame was made up of about 19 pine

The Blackfeet lived in tepees that were easy to put up and move.

Willow backrests were used in Blackfeet tepees.

poles. Each pole was around 18 feet long. The poles were covered with 6 to 20 buffalo skins. These were often decorated with pictures of animals and geometric designs. Furnishings included buffalo robes for beds and willow backrests.

After the buffalo were gone and the reservations were set up, the Blackfeet replaced tepees with log cabins. The log cabin was a symbol of a new, settled way of life.

Clothing

The Blackfeet used buffalo, deer, elk, and antelope skins to make clothing. Women wore ankle-length, sleeveless dresses held up by straps. They were decorated with porcupine quills, cut fringe, and simple designs. In the winter, skin sleeves were added. Buffalo robes also provided warmth. After contact with whites, clothing changed. Women began to use wool and cloth to make many of their garments. The buffalo robe, however, was an important piece of clothing through the 19th century.

Men wore leggings made of antelope skin, moccasins, and shirts. They also wore breechcloths (flaps of material that hung from the waist and covered the front and back). In winter, they wore long buffalo robes. These were often decorated with earth pigments or plant dyes and elaborate porcupine-quill embroidery. During the late 19th century, the Blackfeet were under pressure from missionaries and the loss of the buffalo. As a result, they began to wear what was called "citizen's dress." This outfit was made up of a coat and pants. Because the Blackfeet did not like the whites' stiff shoes, they kept their moccasins.

Buffalo robes were painted and embroidered with porcupine quills.

Blackfeet men usually wore their hair long and loose. Women parted their hair and wore it in long braids. Both men and women often put buffalo fat on their hair to make it shine. They wore necklaces of braided sweetgrass. Men also wore necklaces made from the claws and teeth of bears. Women wore bracelets of elk or deer teeth.

Food

Buffalo was boiled, roasted, or dried. Pieces of fresh meat were cooked with wild roots and vegetables to make a stew. Intestines were cleaned and stuffed with a meat mixture to make a type of sausage.

Pemmican is made from meat and stored in a rawhide bowl.

Dried meat was stored in rawhide pouches or was made into *pemmican* (a food made from dried meat ground into a paste). Men hunted game such as deer, moose, mountain sheep, antelope, and elk. Most Blackfeet thought fish, reptiles, and grizzly bears were unfit for humans to eat.

Blackfeet women gathered roots, prairie turnips, bitterroot, and camas bulbs to add to the diet. They picked wild berries, chokecherries, and buffalo or bull berries. They also used the sweet inside portions of the bark of cottonwood trees.

Education

Blackfeet boys learned how to hunt, track game, and endure physical pain. They also learned how to see signals from both the physical and spiritual worlds. Girls were taught how to make food and clothing, how to sew and do beadwork, and how to dress game and tan hides.

As early as 1859, Roman Catholic missionaries brought Christian religious and educational practices to the Blackfeet. Catholic priests started schools that taught the Indians how to farm and raise cattle. The priests served as go-betweens for the Blackfeet and whites. They learned the Blackfeet language and even translated Christian texts into it.

A Catholic school for Blackfeet students. Catholic missionaires learned the Blackfeet language and served as go-betweens for the the tribes and whites.

The Catholic influence lessened in the early 1900s. At that time, the federal government set up a boarding school and day schools for the Blackfeet. These schools did not allow the children to speak their native language or follow their traditions or religion. Children were punished if they sang Indian songs or did tribal dances. The schools were often overcrowded and dirty.

During the 1960s and 1970s, the Montana Blackfeet encouraged tribal elders to teach their native language and customs to younger people. Blackfeet language and cultural values are taught in Head Start programs on the reservation today. Similar programs have also been created for adults at nearby colleges.

A Blackfeet medicine man received the ability to heal illness through visions.

Healing practices

The Blackfeet believed that spirits were a very real part of everyday life. Illness was seen as the presence of an evil spirit in a person's body. Illness could only be cured by a professional medicine person who had received the ability to heal in a vision. Many Blackfeet doctors were women.

During a healing ceremony, a medicine person might remove some

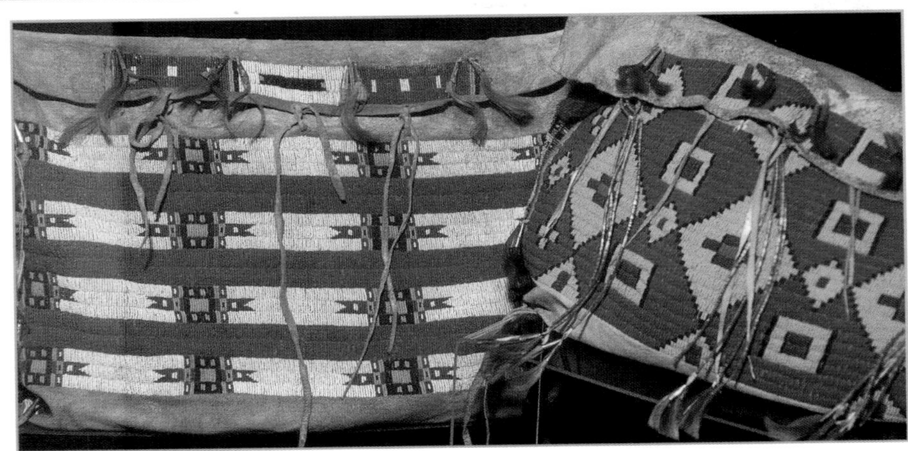

Blackfeet healers used craftwork bags such as these as part of their healing ritual.

object (which the doctor may have brought with him or her) from the sick person. The object was presented as proof that the ceremony had been successful. Healers learned to use natural herbs to treat minor injuries, such as cuts. Horses were often offered as payment for a medicine person's services.

Arts

The Blackfeet were known for their fine craftwork and their beautiful tepees, weapons, and riding equipment. On the reservation, the people used the supplies available to make their goods. For example, they used brass tacks and brass bells to make elaborate beaded headdresses, clothing, and accessories.

Today, there is a Museum of the Plains Indian in Browning, Montana. It features Blackfeet pottery, clothing, art, and moccasins. It displays Blackfeet shields, and jewelry.

CUSTOMS

Gender roles

Some Native American Sun Dancers pierced their skin with sticks and attached the sticks to a pole with ropes.

Unlike many other tribes, the Blackfeet were not strict in their beliefs about what was male or female work. Men sometimes sewed their own clothing. Married women could become healers. Before the 1880s, it was common for a young married woman with no children to go with men to battles, hunts, or on raids. These women mainly prepared food. Sometimes, though, they helped wage war or herd stolen horses back to their tribe.

Festivals and ceremonies

The major religious ceremony, the Sun Dance, was held each year in late summer. First, a Sun Dance lodge was built around a central cottonwood pole in the village. To prepare, dancers made sacred vows and refused both food and water. Then the dance began, and lasted for four days.

Every year, the Blackfeet have a powwow in Browning, Montana.

Dancers sang sacred songs and chants. They also called on the sun to grant them power, luck, or success. Some dancers pierced their skin with sticks. These sticks were then attached to the center pole by rawhide ropes. As they moved, the dancers pulled away from the pole until the sticks tore free. Government officials forbade the Sun Dance in the late-nineteenth and early-twentieth centuries. Even so, it never totally disappeared.

In modern times, Canadian Blackfeet in Alberta sponsor the Blackfoot Indians Art Show at Fort MacLeod. The show features native paintings, beadwork, quillwork, and sculpture. Visitors enjoy a selection of native food. Among the foods available are frybread, buffalo and venison pemmican, griddlecakes, and fine jams and jellies.

Every year, the Blackfeet Powwow is held in Browning, Montana. The four-day celebration

Blackfeet marriages were arranged when the bride was a child.

includes song and dance, stories, drumming, and games. On the menu are native foods. These include boiled beef and deer meat, boiled potatoes, baking powder bread, and frybread. The powwow helps non-natives learn about the ways of the Blackfeet.

Courtship and marriage

Blackfeet marriages were arranged by the bride's parents when she was still a child. Marriage might also be arranged later by close friends or relatives of the couple. Before a wedding could take place, the groom had to convince the bride's father, relatives, or friends that he was worthy. He had to prove that he was able to support his bride. Because of this requirement, very few men married before the age of 21.

Gifts were central to the marriage ceremony. Horses were among the most valuable gifts. The families of the young couple also gave them household goods and robes. After the wedding, the bride and groom lived either in their own hut or in the home of the husband's family.

Funerals

The body of a dead person was sometimes placed between two trees.

Dying people made known who should receive their possessions. When no arrangement was made, members of the tribe simply took whatever they could gather after the person died.

The face of the dead person was painted. The body was dressed in fancy clothes and wrapped in buffalo robes. The corpse was either buried atop a hill or in a ravine, or was placed between the forks of a tree. To mourn the death of loved ones, both men and women cut their hair. They also wore old clothes and smeared their faces with white clay.

When a prominent chief of the Canadian Blackfeet died, his possessions were left within his lodge. His horses were shot. It was believed that the spirit of the deceased did not leave this world. Instead, it traveled to the Sand Hills, an area south of the Saskatchewan River. Invisible spirits of the dead lived there much as they had in life.

Current tribal issues

The Blackfeet have always been concerned about their land. Today, the tribe makes claims for water rights on the reservation. It also claims rights to certain natural resources within the boundaries of Glacier National Park. Members work to make sure that reservation lands are used in appropriate ways.

The Blackfeet want to preserve their culture. Programs have been started to strengthen the sense of community. This may help the Blackfeet overcome social problems such as poverty and crime. The tribe also makes efforts to develop industry, put oil and natural gas resources to use, and maintain ranches on the reservation.

Notable people

At the age of seven, Earl Old Person (1929-) began to present Blackfeet culture in songs and dances at statewide events. For many years, he has served as chairperson of the Blackfeet Tribal Business Council. Under his guidance, many improvements have been made on the reservation. Old Person has also served as head of a number of national native organizations. In 1978, he was given an honorary lifetime appointment as chief of the Blackfeet Nation.

Other notable Blackfeet include: architect Douglas Cardinal (1934-); Blood tribal leader Crowfoot (1830-

1890); Blood politician James Gladstone (1887-1971); painter Gerald Tailfeathers (1925-1975); and Blackfeet/Gros Ventre novelist James Welch (1940-).

James Gladstone

For More Information

Dempsey, Hugh A. *Crowfoot: Chief of the Blackfeet.* Norman: University of Oklahoma Press, 1972.

Ewers, John C. *The Blackfeet: Raiders on the Northwestern Plains.* Norman: University of Oklahoma Press, 1958.

Ewers, John C. *Indian Life on the Upper Missouri.* Norman: University of Oklahoma Press, 1968.

Lacey, Theresa Jensen. *The Blackfeet.* New York: Chelsea House Publishers, 1995.

Society-Blackfoot Web site: http://lucy.ukc.ac.uk/EthnoAtlas/Hmar/Cult_dur/Culture.7833

Glossary

Alliance a group that is formed and who works together for a common cause

Allotment a piece of land given to Native Americans by the government

Drought a long period of time in which there is little to no rainfall or available water

Reservation land set aside and given to Native Americans

Ritual something that is custom or done in a certain way

Sacred highly valued and important

Tame no longer wild, domesticated by humans

Tradition a custom or an established pattern of behavior

Treaty agreement

Tribe a group of people who live together in a community

Index